D0065468

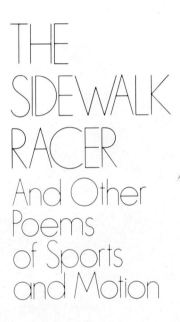

THE SIDEWALK RACER
And Other Poems of Sports and Motion

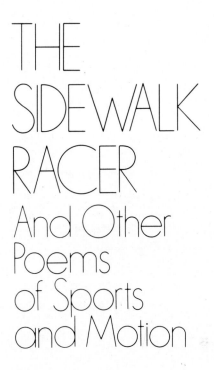

THE SIDEWALK RACER

And Other Poems of Sports and Motion

LILLIAN MORRISON

Lothrop, Lee & Shepard Co.
A Division of William Morrow & Co., Inc.
New York

Library of Congress Cataloging in Publication Data
Morrison, Lillian.
    The sidewalk racer, and other poems of sports and
motion.
    SUMMARY: A collection of poems on sports themes
ranging from professional baseball and boxing to
jumprope and stickball.
    1. Sports—Juvenile poetry.   [1. Sports—Poetry.
2. American poetry]   I. Title.
PZ8.3.M827Si   811'.5'4   77-907
ISBN 0-688-41805-8   ISBN 0-688-51805-2 lib. bdg

ACKNOWLEDGEMENTS
Some of the poems appeared first in the following
publications: *The American Pen:* "The Possessors,"
copyright © 1975 by P.E.N. American Center; *Big Moon
Quarterly:* "Girl-Child" and "Volare"; *Counter/Measures:*
"Rural Recreation," copyright © 1974 by Counter/
Measures; *Poetry Northwest:* "Of Kings and Things"
copyright © 1964 by University of Washington; *Sports
Illustrated:* "Photo Finish" copyright © 1959 by Time,
Inc.; *13th Moon:* "Streetfighter Moon" as "Moon Talking"
copyright © 1974 by *13th Moon; World Tennis:*
"Dis-Play."

"The Boxer," "Night Game," "Posture," and "Sailing,
Sailing" as "From the Block Island Boat" appeared first
in *The Ghosts of Jersey City and Other Poems* copyright
© 1967 by Lillian Morrison.

"Love Fifteen," "Unspelled," "The Women's 400 Meters"
as "The Racers," and "Chico" as "Drum Solo" first
appeared in *Miranda's Music,* by Jean Boudin and
Lillian Morrison, copyright © 1968 by Lillian Morrison.

"The Sprinters" and "In the beginning was the," both
under the pseudonym Lee Murchison and "Tennis
Clinic" as "At the Tennis Clinic" under the pseudonym
I. L. Martin appeared first in *Sprints and Distances*
(Thomas Y. Crowell Company) copyright © 1965 by
Lillian Morrison.

PHOTOGRAPH CREDITS
Page 2: J. W. Moore. Page 13: Rosmarie Hausherr.
Page 17: Cathy Cade. Page 20: J. W. Moore. Page 25:
Hawaii Visitors Bureau Photo. Page 26: Ray Shaw.
Page 31: Austrian National Tourist Office. Page 34:
Rosmarie Hausherr. Page 37: Rosmarie Hausherr.
Page 41: Austrian National Tourist Office. Page 44: June
Harrison. Page 47: Laima Druskis. Page 50: Rosmarie
Hausherr. Page 55: Rosmarie Hausherr. Page 56: J. W.
Moore. Page 61: Rosmarie Hausherr.

To all athletes of street
and sandlot
and especially
to those I played touch-tackle
with on Fleet Street

Contents

Forms of Praise

Basketball players
already tall
rise on springs
aspiring for the ball,
leap for the rebound
arms on high
in a dance
of hallelujahs.

The Sidewalk Racer
or
On the Skateboard

Skimming
an asphalt sea
I swerve, I curve, I
sway; I speed to whirring
sound an inch above the
ground; I'm the sailor
and the sail, I'm the
driver and the wheel
I'm the one and only
single engine
human auto
mobile.

Streetfighter Moon

I take on the whole ocean
I say Come on
throw everything you've got
you can't touch me.
Get mad
I'll stay calm
I'll hypnotize you.
With one arm tied behind me
I'll make you run
from one side of the world
to the other
till you're rocky.

Passing Fair

There is nothing more fair
than to pluck a long forward pass from the air
on a field of grass   except perhaps
to have thrown the pass.

The Women's 400 Meters

Skittish,
they flex knees, drum heels and
shiver at the starting line

waiting the gun
to pour them over the stretch
like a breaking wave.

Bang! they're off
careening down the lanes,
each chased by her own bright tiger.

Rural Recreation

Out here in Ringoes*
I'm hitting fungoes
in my backyard,
a big backyard.
Wherever I go
my brother Bing goes
he likes to sit here
and play the bongos
while I hit fungoes
soft and hard
and so the spring goes
out here in Ringoes.

*Ringoes, New Jersey — Pop. 500

Night Game

At first I thought it was the moon
gliding down with one
shining arm outstretched
carrying something dark.
Then I realized
it was the Statue of Liberty
arcing slowly through the sky
with a baseball glove on her
uplifted hand. She was saying,
"Umpire, you blind burglar,
You can't throw me out of the game."

I Love All Gravity Defiers

The vaulter suspended
on a slender pole
hangs in the air
before his fall.

The trapeze artist
tumbles through space
in split-second rescues
from the abyss.

Kids on swings
pumping to the sky
in a pendulum of pleasure,
fly.

Ski-jumpers, speed-propelled,
extended in flight
loop down
to land upright.

Hail gravity defiers,
jumpers, broad and high
and all non-jumpers
who will not drop, who try.

Somersaulters
on the trampoline,
battered boxers
up at the count of nine

Springboard athletes
jackknifing as they dive
and people who stand straight
and stay alive.

The Sprinters

The gun explodes them.
Pummeling, pistoning they fly
In time's face.
A go at the limit
A terrible try
To smash the ticking glass,
Outpace the beat
That runs, that streaks away
Tireless, and faster than they.

Beside ourselves
(It is for us they run!)
We shout and pound the stands
For one to win
Loving him, whose hard
Grace-driven stride
Most mocks the clock
And almost breaks the bands
Which lock us in.

Tennis Clinic

There was a young man from Port Jervis
Who developed a marvelous service
But was sorry he learned it
For if someone returned it
It made him impossibly nervous.

The Surfer
or
Bliss on a Board

He paddles out,
awaits his chosen wave,
the curling water
that will ride him in.
Spilling, it comes
and he's a water bird
in flight
for thirty seconds.

The Knockout

The shortest fight
I ever saw
Was a left to the body
And a right to the jaw.

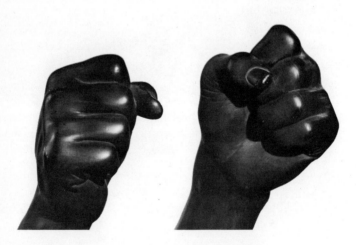

The Boxer

Relentless rat-tat-tat,
thud-thuds, and joggings,
skiprope counterpoint,
precise and swift,
he spars, he is ready.

Enters the ring, near-naked,
alone with his task.

Wham! He rocks you
with a body blow —
dances off, jabs,
moves in again
with pitiless grace
in close, slugging

Uppercut, a left and a right,
hook, feint, clinch
in a square of light
The knockout punch
the old one-two;
and now you know
what you almost knew.

Dis-Play

The doubles partners quarreled so,
The umpire called a halt;
They forfeited the match because
It was their double fault.

On Our Bikes

The roads to the beach
                 are winding
    we glide down
                 breeze-whipped
curving
           past hills of sand
    pedal and coast
                 through wide smell of the sea
                 old familiar sunfeel
       windwallop.

Race you to the water's edge!

Sailing, Sailing
(Lines written to keep the mind
off incipient seasickness)

There is no impeding
That proceeding,
No deflating
That undulating
Or overthrowing
The to-and-froing,
Or undoing
The fro-and-toing,
That silky insisting
Never desisting,
That creasing, uncreasing
Never ceasing,
No deterrence
To the recurrence,
No cessation
To the pulsation,
No stopping the dropping
Of the wave,
The plopping, slopping
Of the foam.
We brave it
Afloat in a boat
On the perpetual
Wet-you-all
(No controlling that rolling)
Motion
Hasten, Jason
Of the ocean.
Get the basin.

Of Kings and Things

What happened to Joey on our block
Who could hit a spaldeen four sewers
And wore his invisible crown
With easy grace, leaning, body-haloed
In the street-lamp night?

He was better than Babe Ruth
Because we could actually see him hit
Every Saturday morning,
With a mop handle thinner than any baseball bat,
That small ball which flew forever.
Whack! straight out at first, then
Rising, rising unbelievably soaring in a
Tremendous heart-bursting trajectory
To come down finally, blocks away,
Bouncing off a parked car's
Fender, eluding the lone outfielder.

Did he get a good job?
Is he married now, with kids?
Is he famous in another constellation?
I saw him with my own eyes in those days
The God of stickball
Disappearing down the street
Skinny and shining in the nightfall light.

Zen and the Art of Golf with Cart

Coasting along in our carts
over waves of green carpet
we are free sailers
and the balls too
will sail free and straight
in the right direction
if we are wise enough
slow enough, devoted enough
to perfection.
so we try. *Head down,*
left arm straight,
easy back swing,
eye on the ball,
CONCENTRATE
then whip it, click,
a winging loop
far far down the fairway.
That was me! Mimi, did you see?
Heart lifts, hills applaud,
full speed ahead in our joyous spurting.
Even the next whiff
will not be hurting
with the memory still in the bones
of the last great smack and trajectory.

The Angels of Motion

When you highjump
hurdle the bar
fling a frisbee
throw a ball
your angels fly.

When you fumble a pass
strike out
break a bone
take a fall

surprised in mid-air,
they droop wings
drop to hover
and fly on with a flutter
but not so high.

Nine Triads
(After the Irish, 9th Century)

Three grand arcs:
 the lift of the pole vaulter over the bar
 the golf ball's flight to the green
 the home run into the bleachers

Three pleasurable curves:
 the ice skater's figure eight
 the long cast of the fisherman
 the arched back of the gymnast

Three swishes that lift the heart:
 the basketball's spin through the net
 the skier's swoop down the snowpacked hill
 the diver's entry into the water

Three glides of satisfaction:
 the ice hockey forward's, after the goal
 the swimmer's turn at the end of the pool
 the finish of the bobsled run

Three swift arrivals to admire:
 the completed pass
 the arrow into the bull's-eye
 the sprinter at the tape

Three shots requiring skill:
 the slapshot
 the shot-put
 the putt out

Three carriers of suspense:
 the place kick for a field goal
 the rim shot
 three balls and two strikes

Three vital sounds:
      the hunter's horn
      the starter's gun
      the bell for the end of the round

Three excellent wishes:
      to move the body with grace
      to fly without a machine
      to outrun time

Surf

Waves want
to be wheels,
They jump for it
and fail
fall flat
like pole vaulters
and sprawl
arms outstretched
foam fingers
reaching.

The Spearthrower

She walks alone
to the edge of the park
and throws into
the bullying dark
her javelin
of light,
her singing sign
her signed song
that the runner may run
far and long
her quick laps
on the curving track
that the sprinter surge
and the hurdler leap
that the vaulter soar,
clear the highest bar,
and the discus fly
as the great crowds cry
to their heroines
Come on!

Out in the Boat

Water lilies,
those big soft jewels
the lake wears,
float in their settings.
Ten ducks sail by — one gondola.
A gull swoops.
The fishing line loops out.
Cast in these waters
with a limber rod
and you'll come up with something
if only the smooth cricket sound
cross-stitching the calm
as you reel in the slack.
Or just sit
as the boat glides.
Other sounds,
the smack of oars,
ripples lapping the sides,
a loon's cry,
stipple the stillness;
and fishing in this quietude
in deeper waters than the lake holds
you may catch some silver beauties,
sunfish of the mind,
whose like has never been seen,
to carry back with you
to cities.

Coastline Olympics

The waves reach up
in limber applause.
They roar
as the ripples
race each other to shore
and crown every winner
with foam.

Beautiful Ben

He wanted
his muscles
to BULGE.
When flexed
the biceps
showed big
and ROUND
abdominals
ridges of iron
pectorals
sturdy mounds.
It did look good.
He was a god
on the beach
supreme
in every tussle
but his heart
was musclebound
and he couldn't
locate the pain.

Love Fifteen

Swing to wallop,
stretch to smash
the bounding ball
O whip it down
and cover the ground
easily, lightly.

Smack the serve
and swift return,
stroke it fine,
drive it deep,
slam the lob's
looping flight,
Whang!

Here within
the chalked white
boundaries of
a sunny world,
test the best,
the body's wit
the body's reach
the body's might

Dancers in
a rigorous rite
who with every
ardent motion
praise the dark
and primal pulse
that pounds and bounces
in the light.

Volare

Catapulted by charm
into a ditch again.
Sometimes I land on my head.

I just love to fly through the air
I love to fly!

Next time I swear
I'll go real high,
skydiver with the perfect parachute,

touch Paradise
before the whammy hits
and come down easy, easy.

Francie

Not a cowboy after all
but the horse,
a restless pony
pawing at the gate
who'll buck and run the hilly range
or skim the straightaway,
fast, semi-tamable,
who'll take a dare,
jump through the plate glass window
anytime you say.

Chico

I'm a sharpshooter
    with a fly swat
I'm a spark footer
    in a jog trot
I'm a scar brooder
    but I try not
I'm a star mover
    with a sky mop.

New Season

Up — with the slap of the sun
do handsprings on the bedsprings
and sail out the window
to the street of the bouncing girls.
I won't go to Macy's any more, more, more,
There's a big, fat policeman at the door, door, door.
Jump high, girls, in the hair-flapping breeze
and the grass will sprout;
Boys, chin the sky bars,
trees will grow tall,
and past the street
in the park of the wet rocks
let all the springs
Gush.

Girl-child

I wish I was
the middleweight champ
of the world,
or a leading contender,
a fasthanded tiger
with good moves,
a TNT punch
and a belly made of rock,
knuckling my nose,
bouncing on my toes,
ambling down the street
past the hustlers on the corner
in a new silk suit, the best.
Wouldn't say a thing,
just wave to the guys,
muscles bulging a little
through the material
of my eighty-dollar jacket,
and inside, the real stuff,
the champ.

Posture

I roamed the streets
dreaming the perfect kayo.
My father driving by
was bothered by my big bouncing strides.

Part of me who lived
in an alley had told me,
Walk close to the walls, Lil,
ready to spring if attacked.

Quick reflexes, fast hands,
high heartbeat, steady, intimate,
soft force of air breathed in and out,
How could the enemy withstand
such readiness?

Unspelled

It is over.
The script uncurls
and I skip rope
in the unraveled letters
of your name.
The line whips
the ground fast
Salt Pepper Vinegar Mustard
I jumpjumpjump
FREE, not missing
a beat, no longer tripping
over Y-O-U.

Fair or Foul

Our lives are loops
or line drives
bunts, grounders, towering
home runs
and death a stumpy shortstop
or a tall guy out in left field
waiting to gather us up.

Photo Finish

Two track stars ran a race
and neither knew defeat.
Both perished at the tape;
they called it a dead heat.

The Possessors

In the muscles of words
expanding, contracting,
I practice.
I feel their pulse
I am embraced by them.

Tongues in your resonant caves
I move and shake with you
to the batter and massage
of consonants
and let the vowels
take me swimming.

I want to flex my x's
tumbling, hum my m's
so tendons tremble and cords agree
though I polish, they possess,
these sounds own me.

The Completion

I've dropped back to pass,
elbow crooked, ready;
the tacklers swarm.
Is there still time
to hit a target?
I snap it swift,
a bullet of love,
from me to you
who rise from the field, turn
in slow motion
and gather it in with ease
in spite of all blockers.

In the beginning was the

Kickoff.
The ball flew
spiralling true
into the end zone
where it was snagged,
neatly hugged
by a swivel-hipped back
who ran up the field
and was smeared.

The game has begun.
The game has been won.
The game goes on.
Long live the game.
Gather and lock
tackle and block
move, move around the arena
and always the beautiful trajectories.

LILLIAN MORRISON is the Coordinator of Young Adult Services for the New York Public Library. The author of two volumes of poetry, she is also represented in many anthologies. She is well-known for her collections of folk rhymes and for *Sprints and Distances,* the highly acclaimed anthology of sports poetry.

Of *The Sidewalk Racer* Ms. Morrison says, "I love rhythms, the body movement implicit in poetry, explicit in sports. I have always believed that the attempt to achieve excellence in either of these fields is both noble and exciting. And there are emotions connected with sports, sometimes a kind of transcendence and beauty one wants to catch. One turns naturally to poetry to express these things."